DATE DUE

			PRINTED IN U.S.A.

JENNIFER
LAWRENCE
STAR OF *THE HUNGER GAMES*

JENNIFER LAWRENCE

STAR OF *THE HUNGER GAMES*

Katherine Krohn

LERNER PUBLICATIONS COMPANY • MINNEAPOLIS

Lerner Publications Company
A division of Lerner Publishing Group, Inc.
241 First Avenue North
Minneapolis, MN U.S.A. 55401

Website address: www.lernerbooks.com

Library of Congress Cataloging-in-Publication Data

Krohn, Katherine E.
    Jennifer Lawrence : star of *the hunger games* / by Katherine Krohn.
       p.   cm. — (Gateway biographies)
    Includes bibliographical references and index.
    ISBN 978-0-7613-8642-1 (lib. bdg. : alk. paper)
      1. Lawrence, Jennifer, 1990- —Juvenile literature. 2. Actors—United States—
Biography—Juvenile literature. I. Title.
    PN2287.L28948K86 2012
    791.4302'8092—dc23 [B]   2011030785

Manufactured in the United States of America
1 – BP – 12/31/11

The images in this book are used with the permission of: © Gabriel Bouys/AFP/Getty Images, p. 2; © iStockphoto.com/Susan Trigg, pp. 3, 6 (background), 26, 33; AP Photo/ Evan Agostini, p. 6; © Kevin Winter/Getty Images, p. 9; Seth Poppel Yearbook Library, pp. 10, 11; © Fred Hayes/Getty Images, p. 12; © David Coleman/Alamy, p. 14; © Frazer Harrison/Getty Images, p. 16; Danny Feld/© TBS/Courtesy Everett Collection, p. 17; © Phase 4 Films/Courtesy Everett Collection, p. 19; © Alberto Pizzoli/AFP/Getty Images, p. 20; © Roadside Attractions/Courtesy Everett Collection, p. 22; Ken Regan/© Summit Entertainment/Courtesy Everett Collection, p. 25; Murray Close/TM and Copyright © 20th Century Fox Film Corp. All rights reserved/Courtesy Everett Collection, p. 27; © Robyn Beck/AFP/Getty Images, p. 28; © Dan MacMedan/WireImage/Getty Images, p. 30; Jeff Malet Photography/Newscom, p. 32; © Jason Merritt/Getty Images, p. 34; © Steve Granitz/WireImage/Getty Images, p. 36; Greg Allen/Rex USA, p. 37; Lloyd Bishop/NBCU Photo Bank via AP Images, p. 38.
Front Cover: © Marcel Thomas/FilmMagic/Getty Images; © iStockphoto.com/Susan Trigg (background)
Main body text set it Rotif Serif Std 55 Regular 14/17
Typeface provided by Agfa

CONTENTS

Jennifer Lawrence attends an awards celebration in 2011. Jennifer was selected to play the role of Katniss in the movie based on the popular book *The Hunger Games*.

Dear Readers: We have found Katniss," announced Suzanne Collins, author of *The Hunger Games*, in March 2011 in a statement to the press. Jennifer Lawrence had been selected to play the starring role of Katniss Everdeen in the upcoming movie based on Collins's books.

The Hunger Games story is set in a dark and desperate future time. Young people are forced to fight one another to the death on an annual reality TV show. The broad popularity of *The Hunger Games* is similar to that of Stephenie Meyer's *Twilight* series and J. K. Rowling's Harry Potter books.

Jennifer Lawrence was a huge *Hunger Games* fan before she auditioned for the role. "I couldn't be happier about being a part of *Hunger Games* and play[ing] Katniss," she announced.

Many people were happy with the decision to cast Jennifer as Katniss. Jennifer had shown her ability to play a strong young woman in films such as *The Poker House* and *Winter's Bone*. But not everyone was thrilled with the decision. *Hunger Games* fans vented their

THE HUNGER GAMES

New York Times Bestselling Author

SUZANNE COLLINS

The movie *The Hunger Games* is based on this book by Suzanne Collins. The book has enjoyed worldwide popularity, much like the *Twilight* series has in recent years.

feelings on social networking websites such as Twitter and Facebook.

"She's a HORRIBLE match for Katniss," commented a reader on Facebook's official *Hunger Games* page. "The book said she had olive skin, dark hair, and gray eyes. Jennifer? Blonde hair, pale skin, blue eyes. WHYYY???!!"

Hunger Games director, Gary Ross, acknowledged that fans felt "very passionately that their take on the character is unique and correct." But for Ross, the choice was clear. Casting Jennifer as Katniss "was the easiest casting decision I ever made in my life," he said.

Suzanne Collins also felt strongly that Jennifer was perfect for the part. "I never thought we'd find somebody

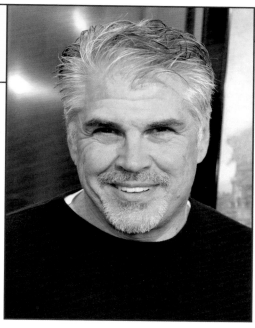

Gary Ross, director of *The Hunger Games,* selected Jennifer to play the part of Katniss.

this amazing for the role," said Collins. "And I can't wait for everyone to see her play it."

KENTUCKY GIRL

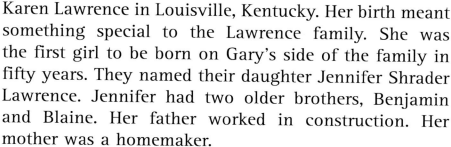

On August 15, 1990, a baby girl was born to Gary and Karen Lawrence in Louisville, Kentucky. Her birth meant something special to the Lawrence family. She was the first girl to be born on Gary's side of the family in fifty years. They named their daughter Jennifer Shrader Lawrence. Jennifer had two older brothers, Benjamin and Blaine. Her father worked in construction. Her mother was a homemaker.

As a young girl, Jennifer did her best to keep up with her big brothers. They taught her to fish and wrestle. Ben and Blaine were both athletic and played sports. Jennifer wasn't as interested in sports. But she had lots of energy, and playing games such as basketball and softball was fun for her. "We nicknamed her 'Nitro' because she was so hyper," recalled Ben.

Jennifer had a quiet side too. She was a good student and earned good grades. She also liked to draw and to play the guitar. Once she got in trouble for sticking gum under the living room table. But she rarely acted up. "She liked to be with her easel and books. She had places in her mind to go," said her mom.

The worlds of books, movies, and TV shows fascinated Jennifer. "I've just always loved stories, in any way, shape, or form," she says. "If I was in the car and I had no way to [read or watch TV], my parents had to tell me one story after another."

The Lawrence family attended church, and Jennifer enjoyed acting in church plays. She liked how she could use her imagination to make a character come alive. Acting felt natural to Jennifer. She told her parents that she wanted to become an actor. Karen and Gary Lawrence weren't sure what to think. They knew Jennifer was talented. But they figured she was probably just going through a phase.

Jennifer Lawrence in her seventh-grade class photo. In sixth grade, she was voted most talkative.

In seventh grade, Jennifer *(top left)* was on the Kammerer Middle School cheerleading squad.

Jennifer went to Kammerer Middle School in Louisville. The brick building on Wesboro Road was home to the Kammerer Cubs. At Kammerer, Jennifer found an outlet for her energy on the school cheerleading squad.

Jennifer loved being at the center of things. She liked school and continued to get good grades. But her desire to become a professional actor stayed with her.

In 2004 fourteen-year-old Jennifer got an idea. Spring break from school was coming up. She begged her mom to take her to New York City. Jennifer knew New York was a center for the entertainment industry. She wanted to spend her break applying at acting and modeling agencies.

Karen wasn't sure what to do. She knew how determined her daughter could be. After thinking it over, she decided to take her to New York. Once there, Karen figured, Jennifer would see how hard it is to find work as an actress. After all, millions of hopeful actors had made a similar trip to New York in search of an acting career. She figured visiting New York might just put an end to Jennifer's obsession with becoming an actor.

What Jennifer's mom didn't know is that her daughter's life was about to change. There was no stopping Jennifer when she had her mind set on something.

Jennifer *(far left)* sits next to her mother, Karen Lawrence, at a brunch during a film festival. Karen brought Jennifer to New York in 2004 to see if Jennifer could find work as an actress.

In April 2004, Jennifer and her mom walked out of a talent agency in New York City. Jennifer was thrilled. She had just completed her first cold read. (A cold read is when a person acts from a script that he or she hasn't previously seen.) Jennifer was sure the audition had gone well. In fact, the agency staff told her it was the best cold read they had ever heard by someone her age.

Although the reading had gone well, Karen still had her doubts. She felt protective of her daughter and didn't want anyone to take advantage of her. "My mom told me they were lying," Jennifer later recalled. "My parents were the exact opposite of stage parents. They did everything in their power to keep [my acting career] from happening. But it was going to happen no matter what. I was like, 'Thanks for raising me, but I'm going to take it from here.'"

That afternoon Jennifer and her mom explored New York City. The streets were alive with activity and all kinds of people. Union Square, at the intersection of Broadway and 4th Avenue, was a popular gathering spot. Strolling through Union Square, Jennifer and her mom saw a commercial being filmed. They stopped to watch dancers performing in the commercial. While they watched, Jennifer noticed a man staring at her. He came up to her and asked if he could take her picture. He was a talent agent, he explained. He was involved with the commercial being filmed. He seemed professional,

Jennifer and her mom were in Union Square *(above)* in New York when a talent agent approached. He wanted to take Jennifer's picture and to invite her to an audition at his agency.

so Jennifer and her mom agreed. After taking Jennifer's photograph, the man asked for Karen's phone number.

The man called the next day. He wanted Jennifer to come to his talent agency for a cold read. Like the first agency where Jennifer had done a cold read, this second agency was very impressed. They were interested in working with Jennifer. But for that to happen, Jennifer would have to stay in New York for the summer.

Jennifer's parents weren't sure about the idea. But Jennifer's brothers, Ben and Blaine, were supportive. They reminded their parents how Jennifer had gone to every football and baseball game of theirs. They pointed out that "*this* [acting] is her football field or baseball diamond."

Jennifer's parents decided to get a professional acting teacher's thoughts on their daughter's potential. They took her to see Flo Greenberg, a well-known acting coach. After seeing Jennifer act, Greenberg had a strong opinion. "I was eager for her to pursue her acting career immediately," she said. "I don't say that about many people. Sometimes you need to know when to keep your hands off and let somebody's natural technique blossom."

Encouraged, the Lawrences decided to rent an apartment in New York for two months. Jennifer's parents took turns staying with her and supervising her career. "I knew she was serious about this because she never complained [about the hard work involved in an acting career]," said her father.

In the following weeks, modeling and talent agencies contacted Jennifer. She did a photo shoot for the clothing line Abercrombie & Fitch. She landed roles in a Burger King commercial and an ad for the MTV reality drama series *My Super Sweet 16*.

Soon after her move to New York, Jennifer signed with a talent agent. Near the end of the summer, her agency flew her to Los Angeles for a screen test. Jennifer got a small part in a movie called *Devil You Know* and minor roles in TV programs such as *Monk* and *Medium*.

At summer's end, fifteen-year-old Jennifer headed back to Kentucky. Though she had returned home, she

Josh Hutcherson is another famous actor from Kentucky.

had no intention of giving up on acting. "I never considered that I wouldn't be successful," said Jennifer. "The phrase 'if it doesn't work out' never popped into my mind."

While Jennifer was reading the newspaper one day, she saw an article that caught her eye. The article was about Josh Hutcherson, a young actor who was also from Kentucky. Hutcherson had recently found fame after appearing in the movie *Little Manhattan*. Jennifer showed her parents the article. "See?" she said. "He's from Kentucky and he made it. I can do it too."

After Jennifer's parents read the story about Hutcherson, something came together for them. The story helped them accept what Jennifer wanted to do with her life. "We would have destroyed her had we not let her follow her dreams," her mother told *Louisville Magazine* journalist Josh Moss.

Gary and Karen struck a deal with Jennifer. She could pursue her acting goals *if* she finished high school. But although she was bound for Ballard High School in

Louisville in September, Jennifer knew that high school wasn't where she needed to be. She had earned a 3.9 grade point average at Kammerer Middle School. At fifteen, Jennifer took the GED exam (a test that people can take to get a diploma without finishing school). She easily passed the exam and earned her diploma. "Some people think I missed out," Jennifer later said. "[But] I got the childhood of my dreams."

Talent agencies stayed in touch with Jennifer. One day an agent called and offered her a role on a new TBS sitcom called *The Bill Engvall Show*. Her parents

Jennifer poses with the rest of the cast of *The Bill Engvall Show* in 2007. From left: Bill Engvall, Nancy Travis, Jennifer Lawrence, Skyler Gisondo, and Graham Patrick Martin.

decided to move the family to California. They bought a condominium in Santa Monica, near Los Angeles where the show was being taped. Jennifer's acting career was on its way!

RISING STAR

On *The Bill Engvall Show*, comedian Bill Engvall played a family counselor who had his own family issues to deal with. Jennifer played Lauren Pearson, Bill's oldest child. She liked joking around with her fellow cast members. They became like a family to her.

In between seasons of the show, Jennifer had time to devote to other projects. She auditioned for all kinds of roles. She even tried out for parts in the movie *Twilight*, including that of the lead character, Bella. Jennifer was never sad when she didn't get a particular part. She believed that whatever was meant to happen would happen. As fate would have it, agents seemed to think Jennifer was better suited for a different kind of role—in dark, serious, independent films. (An independent film, or "indie," is an artistic and typically lower-budget film.)

In 2007 Jennifer landed roles in two independent films, *The Poker House* and *The Burning Plain*. Jennifer strongly related to the character she played in the latter film. "I was kind of going through that turning-into-a-woman phase and discovering what it was like to be a woman . . . and that was kind of what was happening to

Jennifer plays the part of Agnes in the movie *The Poker House* (2008). She won an Outstanding Performance Award at the Los Angeles Film Festival for her role.

my character in the movie," said Jennifer. Critics gave *The Burning Plain* lukewarm reviews. But they praised Jennifer's performance.

The next year, Jennifer was honored with an Outstanding Performance Award at the Los Angeles Film Festival for her performance in *The Poker House.* She was also honored with a Marcello Mastroianni Award for Best New Young Actress at the Venice Film Festival for her work in *The Burning Plain.*

At the 2008 Venice Film Festival, Jennifer picked up the Marcello Mastroianni Award for Best New Young Actress.

Jennifer was discovering herself as an actor. And she was beginning to realize that she didn't want to be labeled as a particular kind of actor. "I just don't like that you can either be ugly and smart or pretty and dumb, or ugly and nice or pretty and mean," she told a reporter. "It's in every studio film you see. There's not a lot of imagination out there. Nobody outside of indie films steps outside the box. That drives me nuts."

In 2009 *The Bill Engvall Show* was canceled. Though Jennifer had loved being part of the show, she was relieved. She was ready to devote herself entirely to film work. Meanwhile, Jennifer's agent sent her a script for an independent film called *Winter's Bone*. Jennifer would be auditioning for the part of Ree Dolly. Ree was a seventeen-year-old who goes in search of her drug addict father to save her family and their home.

"I'd have walked through hot coals to get the part. I thought it was the best female role I'd read—ever," said Jennifer. "I was so impressed by Ree's tenacity and that she didn't take no for an answer."

Jennifer auditioned twice for the role in Los Angeles. Though she had proven herself to be a serious actress, the casting agents weren't sure she *looked* right for the part. Auditions for the film were being held in New York as well. The film's director, Debra Granik, would be at those auditions. Jennifer wanted to show her that she was more than a beautiful face.

Determined to get the role, Jennifer flew overnight from California to New York. She arrived at the audition looking tired and disheveled. She hadn't washed her hair in a week, and she didn't wear makeup. As Jennifer read from the script, she let her acting instincts lead her. Director Granik and producer Anne Rosellini were impressed with Jennifer's natural talent. She had a fierce determination in her eyes when she acted the role of Ree. And there was a depth to her personality that made her seem older than her years. "She looked very physical and athletic, which we always imagined Ree would be, and she had a great voice—a sort of deep earthy tone quality," said Rosellini. "We knew she didn't sleep much [on the flight], and that may have brought an air of desperation or of haggardness to her that maybe a normal 18-year-old wouldn't have."

Jennifer was thrilled when Granik offered her the role. To prepare for the part, Jennifer practiced chopping wood and learned to shoot a gun. In February 2009, filming on *Winter's Bone* began in the Ozark Plateau region of Missouri.

Granik had made an open casting call in the nearby town of Branson, Missouri. Hundreds of locals showed up to try out for small parts in the film. Some Missouri residents landed bigger parts, such as Lauren Sweetser who played Ree's best friend, Gail. On the set, Jennifer and Lauren became close and remained good friends after the production.

The weather in Missouri was bitterly cold. Jennifer typically put in about eighteen hours of work each day. She appeared in every scene in the movie. While shooting the film

In the movie *Winter's Bone* (2010), Jennifer plays the part of Ree Dolly.

was hard, Jennifer loved her work too much to complain.

In one scene, Ree kills and skins a squirrel to help feed her family and to teach her younger brother and sister how to survive. How did she prepare for that scene? "My brother's friend came over with a squirrel he'd shot and we skinned it in my backyard," Jennifer said. While she made skinning a squirrel look easy in the film, shooting the scene was difficult for her. As soon as the scene ended, Jennifer started jumping up and down, screaming in horror.

Some people think Jennifer must be serious and intense to play dark roles like those in *The Burning Plain* or *Winter's Bone.* In real life, Jennifer is fun-loving and lighthearted. While some scenes are very serious, they never leave her feeling drained.

Many actors do "method" acting. That means they bring up feelings from their own past to help them play a part. Jennifer's acting technique is different. She uses her imagination. "If it ever came down to the point where, to make a part better, I had to lose a little bit of my sanity, I wouldn't do it," Jennifer said. "I would just do comedies."

Though Jennifer didn't bring her real emotions to the role, she did have trouble leaving the character of Ree behind. "I knew her inside and out," Jennifer told *USA Today.* "What's weird about wrapping a movie is you spend so much time creating a whole other person, then all [of a] sudden you leave. You stop. And that part of your brain, or head, or imagination, doesn't exist anymore."

Movie critics raved about Jennifer's performance in *Winter's Bone. Rolling Stone* critic Peter Travers wrote that "Lawrence's performance is more than acting, it's a gathering storm. He called Jennifer's eyes "a road map to what's tearing Ree apart."

Jennifer's parents were proud of her—and not just because of her success and talent. "The thing we're most proud of is when we go on set with these people who are around her eighteen hours a day," said her mom. "They see who she really is—they say she's gracious, down-to-earth."

AWARD WINNER

Jennifer's success in *Winter's Bone* brought her new fans, both outside the movie industry and within it. In 2009 director and actor Jodie Foster chose nineteen-year-old Jennifer to play the part of Norah in the dark comedy *The Beaver.* While Foster (who directed and acted in the film) had admired Jennifer's work in *Winter's Bone*, at first she wasn't sure if Jennifer could play a comedic role. "Jodie . . . thought I was too dark," remembered Jennifer. "So I had to fly on another red-eye [all-night flight] to prove I'm funny. I just showed up and made some jokes. Red-eyes always seem to do the trick."

In the quirky movie, Jennifer's character, Norah, is a cheerleader and high school valedictorian. Mel Gibson played the lead role of a depressed toy manufacturer, and Anton Yelchin played Norah's love interest. Jennifer was thrilled to work with Jodie Foster. Foster, like Jennifer, had started her career at an early age. "We both walked away thinking the same thing: 'I've never met anybody who reminds me of me more,'" remarked Jennifer.

Working with Jodie Foster helped Jennifer adjust to the pressures that come with fame. "Honestly, seeing her gave me hope that I could be not only nice, but *normal*," Jennifer said on the TV talk show *Live! with Regis and Kelly*. "She's brilliant. But she's just so normal."

In 2009, Jodie Foster *(right)* worked with Jennifer *(center)* and Anton Yelchin *(left)* on the set of *The Beaver*.

ACTORS SHE ADMIRES

Jennifer Lawrence admires many actors. But she especially likes the work of these actors:

- Alec Baldwin
- Cate Blanchett
- Jeff Bridges
- Jodie Foster
- James Franco
- Michelle Williams

As Jennifer's career evolved, she continued to make an effort to not be seen as any particular type of actor. In May 2010, *Esquire* magazine featured a glamorous and seductive photo spread of Jennifer. She wanted to show the public that she was multidimensional and not just a "troubled tomboy in dark dramas."

In 2010 Jennifer acted in another independent film, *Like Crazy*, directed by Drake Doremus. She also landed a role in *X-Men: First Class*, a Hollywood feature film (a film advertised or presented as a special attraction). Based on a comic book, the movie featured Jennifer as the shape-shifting mutant known as Raven/Mystique.

Getting into character for the role of Raven/Mystique meant more than learning her lines. It took a

Covered in blue makeup, Jennifer *(second from right)* played Raven/ Mystique in the movie ***X-Men: First Class*** (2011).

team of seven makeup artists eight hours to put on her blue, full-body makeup. To pass the time while the paint was applied and dried, Jennifer talked to her girlfriends on the crew, watched reruns of *Sex and the City*, and rewatched favorite movies such as *Dumb and Dumber* and *The Big Lebowski*. "It was like a really bizarre sleepover where I was standing up naked being painted and scaled and glued," noted Jennifer.

During the filming of *X-Men: First Class*, Jennifer lived in London for five months. She rented an apartment in London's Notting Hill district. "The whole cast, we all legitimately love each other," Jennifer said of the time she spent with fellow cast members while filming. "We got addicted to hanging out."

Meanwhile, Jennifer enjoyed acclaim from her past projects. In 2010 *Winter's Bone* won the Grand Jury Prize at the Sundance Film Festival. When Jennifer found out the film had won the prestigious prize, she "just started bawling," she recalled. "I had such an 'actress' moment."

In January 2011, she received more exciting news. She had been nominated for an Academy Award for her role in *Winter's Bone.* At twenty, Jennifer was the second-youngest actress to receive a nomination for Best Performance by an Actress in a Leading Role.

Actress Mo'Nique *(left)* and Academy of Motion Pictures Arts and Sciences president Tom Sherak announce the nominees for Best Actress for the Academy Awards in 2011. The nominees included Jennifer (pictured at the center of the screen) for her role in **Winter's Bone**.

(Keisha Castle-Hughes was the youngest nominee for her performance in *Whale Rider* in 2002.)

Around that same time, Jennifer also received another big honor, a Golden Globe Award nomination for her performance in the film. She was nominated for Best Performance in a Motion Picture (Drama), along with Michelle Williams, Halle Berry, Nicole Kidman, and Natalie Portman. Jennifer's family was very proud of her. "It's amazing to turn on the news to see her being mentioned with Natalie Portman [and] Nicole Kidman," said Jennifer's brother Ben.

In the days leading up to the award ceremonies, Jennifer felt nervous. She also reported feeling like a "rag doll" when hair and makeup professionals showed up at her home to ready her for the events. "They [put] me in new, uncomfortable, weird dresses and expensive shoes," said Jennifer, "and I just shut down and raised my arms up for them to get the dress on and pouted my lips when they needed to put the lipstick on."

On January 16, 2011, Jennifer and her mom attended the 68th Golden Globe Awards in Beverly Hills, California. Jennifer made a bold statement on the red carpet at the ceremony. She wore a Louis Vuitton black flamenco-style gown and her hair in a glamorous updo.

Natalie Portman won the Golden Globe that evening for her role as ballerina Nina Sayers in *Black Swan*. But Jennifer wasn't upset or surprised. Many people had predicted that Portman would take the award. Jennifer felt awestruck when she saw all the famous people at

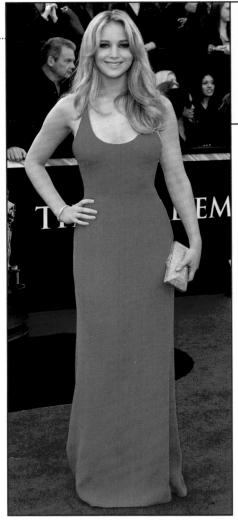

The red Calvin Klein Collection dress that Jennifer wore to the Academy Awards in 2011 was one of the most talked-about fashions of the night. Jennifer appeared on many best-dressed lists.

the award show's after-party. When she saw stars such as Brad Pitt, Angelina Jolie, and Tilda Swinton, she thought to herself, "I'm not cool enough to be at this party. Somebody's made a mistake."

On February 27, 2011, Jennifer attended the 83rd Academy Awards in Los Angeles with her father. She wore a bright red, sleeveless Calvin Klein Collection dress made by designer Francisco Costa. The simple construction of the dress suited Jennifer's no-frills per-sonality and athletic build.

Though Jennifer didn't win an Oscar (the Academy Award trophy) that evening (losing again to Portman), she was thrilled to attend the awards show. She especially enjoyed a performance by the British band Florence and the Machine. "I loved being able to sit next to my dad," said Jennifer. "We just kept looking at each other like, 'I can't believe this is happening.'"

In 2011 Jennifer's schedule was jam-packed. She made TV appearances to promote *X-Men: First Class* and *The Beaver*. She auditioned for new projects too and won a role in her first horror film, *House at the End of the Street.*

When *X-Men: First Class* came to theaters in the summer of 2011, it received excellent reviews. Jennifer's old fans were wowed, and she won new fans too. On Facebook, a viewer commented, "Just watched *X-Men: First Class* and you were SO AWESOME!!!! You were breathtaking and practically every single good adjective listed in the dictionary!"

Does Jennifer prefer working in independent films or big Hollywood productions? "It's all filmmaking," Jennifer told the *Washington Post*. "The behind-the-scenes is always different. You have a bigger trailer, there's better food [with a big-budget film]." Jennifer chooses to do a movie—whether it's big-budget or independent—because she likes the script, the character, and the director or actors involved. She says it is "kind of like camping versus going to a resort. They're both fun; they're just different kinds of fun."

Despite her busy schedule, in 2011 Jennifer had her eye on another movie script. It fit all of her requirements. She loved the script and the character especially. A new, major role was up for grabs in Hollywood—and Jennifer wanted it badly.

CASTING CALL: KATNISS!

From the moment she heard that the book *The Hunger Games* was going to be a movie, Jennifer wanted the leading role of seventeen-year-old Katniss. "I met with [director] Gary Ross, and we had a very long, nice meeting before the audition," she recalled. "And then by the time the audition came around, we were familiar with each other."

The Hunger Games is set in the future in a place called Panem, a nation surrounded by twelve districts. There, in an annual televised event, one randomly selected boy and girl from each district are forced to fight each other to the death.

Suzanne Collins wrote the books as a trilogy (series of three books). The first book is called *The Hunger Games. Catching Fire* is the second, and *Mockingjay* is the third. The books were slated to be made into four movies.

Author Suzanne Collins holds up the final book in *The Hunger Games* series, *Mockingjay*.

THE STORY BEHIND
THE HUNGER GAMES BOOKS

One evening in the early 2000s, novelist and television writer Suzanne Collins was watching TV and flipping through the channels. One program showed young people vying for a prize in a reality game show. Another featured coverage of the Iraq war and showed young people fighting. Because Collins was sleepy, the two programs began to mix together in her mind, and she got an idea for a new novel—about teenagers who fight to the death on a reality show.

From an early age, Collins understood the seriousness of war. Her father was a soldier in the Vietnam War (1957–1975). While he was in Vietnam, whenever she saw coverage of the Vietnam War on TV, she felt terrified. Collins intended her *Hunger Games* books to not only entertain but to make young people think. The books evoke important issues, such as the harsh realities of war.

In an interview with *School Library Journal*, Collins discussed how modern kids are exposed to so much information in the media. She voiced concern that they might get desensitized to reality. "If you're watching a sitcom, that's fine," she says. "But if there's a real-life tragedy unfolding, you should not be thinking of yourself as an audience member. Because those are real people on the screen, and they're not going away when the commercials start to roll."

34

Some people were hoping that *True Grit* actress Hailee Steinfeld would play the role of Katniss.

Besides Jennifer, many top Hollywood actresses wanted the role of Katniss. Fans of *The Hunger Games* felt strongly about who Ross should choose to play the part. While some fans thought Jennifer Lawrence would be great in the role, others worried that she was too blonde, too pretty, or too old to play Katniss. Fan favorites included Hailee Steinfeld and Chloë Moretz.

No matter who the fans thought would make the best Katniss, the final choice was up to Ross. Many hopeful actresses and *Hunger Games* fans awaited his decision.

THE HUNGER GAMES

In March 2011, Ross announced who would play Katniss. It was Jennifer Lawrence! Ross said he was excited to work with Jennifer and watch her bring Katniss to life. "Katniss requires a young actress with strength, depth, complexity, tenderness, and power," said Ross. "There are very few people alive who can bring that to a role. She's going to be an amazing Katniss."

Jennifer felt a mixture of excitement and anxiety about winning the role. "I know from the bottom of my heart that I love Katniss," Jennifer told writer Karen Valby of *Entertainment Weekly*. "It's kind of like when you have a huge crush on somebody, and it's almost scary because you don't want to mess it up and have it not be everything you hope it will be."

Jennifer knew that this role could be the biggest challenge thus far in her career. Her life was about to change dramatically. The next four years would be spent in a whirlwind of movie production and promotional tours. Could she handle being thrown in the media spotlight? Could she handle the fame? Playing the part of Katniss would be challenging both physically and mentally.

"I have a huge responsibility to the fans of this incredible book, and I don't take it lightly," Jennifer told the press four days after the casting decision. "I will give everything I have to these movies and to this role to make it worthy of Suzanne Collins's masterpiece."

In the coming weeks, the rest of *The Hunger Games* cast members were announced. Actor Donald Sutherland was chosen to play the part of evil President Snow. Musician Lenny Kravitz landed the part of Cinna, Katniss's stylist. Coincidentally, Kravitz had already met Jennifer Lawrence. His daughter, Zoë, was also in the cast of *X-Men: First Class.* She and Jennifer had become good friends and spent time hanging out at his home in Paris during breaks from filming in London.

The cast also included Elizabeth Banks (as Effie) and Woody Harrelson (as Haymitch). Stanley Tucci and Jack Quaid (son of Dennis Quaid and Meg Ryan) joined the cast too.

Hunger Games fans were especially interested in what actors would be chosen to play the costarring roles of Peeta and Gale, Katniss's love interests in the film. Ironically, Josh Hutcherson, the young actor from Kentucky, was chosen to play Peeta. Liam Hemsworth would play Gale. How did Jennifer feel about the casting?

"Josh is so charming. He's *so* charming," she says. "But he's [also] sweet, he's down to earth. He embodies all of it and brings it all to Peeta."

Jennifer also had good things to say about Liam Hemsworth. "Liam is just a solid brick of muscle,

Liam Hemsworth was chosen to play Gale, one of Katniss's love interests in **The Hunger Games**.

and you look at him and you're like 'Oh, okay, great!' " remarked Jennifer. "But he's got depth and he's interesting and at the same time he's natural and he flows."

In May 2011, Jennifer Lawrence appeared on the cover of *Entertainment Weekly* as the character Katniss. She looked strong and slender, with a dark tan and dyed brown hair.

Dying her hair was Jennifer's easiest preparation for the role. Like Katniss, Jennifer needed to be in excellent physical condition. For several weeks, before production began at the end of May 2011 in North Carolina, Jennifer did intense physical training for the part.

Because Katniss was excellent with a bow and arrow, Jennifer needed to be too. She spent more than a month working on her archery skills, coached by a four-time Olympian from eastern Europe.

Jennifer waves to fans after an appearance on the *Late Show with David Letterman* in 2011. Jennifer dyed her hair brown for the role of Katniss.

Jennifer practiced tree and rock climbing and running. She learned combat and vaulting. Jennifer also practiced yoga to "stay cat-like."

SKY'S THE LIMIT

Besides acting, preparing for roles, and reading new scripts, Jennifer's days are filled with photo shoots and interviews with the media. But she'd much rather be acting than doing interviews. Like everyone, Jennifer has good days and bad days. Sometimes it's hard to do yet

Jennifer Lawrence does many photo shoots and interviews. Here she is seen on *Late Night with Jimmy Fallon* in 2011 talking about *The Hunger Games*, *X-Men: First Class*, and her new hair color.

another interview when she's not in the mood. "[One day] I had to do an interview," Jennifer recalled. "I was in a horrible mood. I couldn't think of basic words. I could see my publicist in the background, mouthing things to say. They want you to be likeable all the time, and I'm just not."

Jennifer has a home in the Los Angeles area and also keeps an apartment in New York. *Manhattan Movie Magazine* asked her if she did different things in California and New York. "Well, L.A. is where I do my business," she said. "I did learn to surf in L.A. And my friends are different in L.A. They're more musicians and hippies who kind of live on the beach. In New York, they're more hippies that are into fashion."

Jennifer fell in love with London when she filmed *X-Men: First Class* there. She'd like to buy a home in London as well—and perhaps raise a family there one day.

Jennifer is excited about her life. "Mostly, I'm just really happy that I've been able to do what I love," she says. "I know that sounds kind of simple, but I've found something I really love doing and I can do it every day of my life."

For now, her work in *The Hunger Games* movies is keeping her very busy. But eventually, she says, she'd like to be a director. Determined and ambitious, Jennifer Lawrence seems destined for a bright future. "I'm a hard worker, and when I set my mind to something, it usually happens," she says.

IMPORTANT DATES

1990   Jennifer Shrader Lawrence is born in Louis-
        ville, Kentucky, on August 15.

2004   She persuades her mom to take her to New
        York City during her middle school's spring
        break to apply at acting and modeling
        agencies.

2005   She lands jobs as an actor in commercials.

2006   She appears in an episode of the TV show
        Monk.

2007   She appears in an episode of the TV show
        Medium. She also joins the cast of the TBS
        sitcom *The Bill Engvall Show*. Her parents
        move the family to California to be closer to
        Jennifer's work.

        She is chosen for roles in the films *The
        Poker House* and *The Burning Plain*.

2008   She appears in another episode of *Medium*.
        She also wins an Outstanding Performance
        Award at the Los Angeles Film Festival for
        her performance in *The Poker House*. In
        addition, she is honored with a Marcello

Mastroianni Award for Best New Young Actress at the Venice Film Festival for her work in *The Burning Plain*.

2009	*The Bill Engvall Show* is canceled.
	Jennifer travels to the Ozark Plateau region of Missouri to act in the film *Winter's Bone*.
	She is selected to play the part of Norah in the dark comedy *The Beaver*.
2010	She lands the role of Raven/Mystique in *X-Men: First Class*. She lives in London for five months during the filming of the movie.
	Winter's Bone wins the Grand Jury Prize at the Sundance Film Festival.
2011	Jennifer is nominated for an Academy Award and a Golden Globe Award.
	She wins the role of Katniss Everdeen in *The Hunger Games*.
2012	*The Hunger Games* is scheduled for release.

SOURCE NOTES

7   Darren Franich, " 'Hunger Games': Suzanne Collins Talks Jennifer Lawrence as Katniss—EXCLUSIVE," *Entertainment Weekly*, 2011, http://insidemovies.ew.com/2011/03/21/hunger-games-suzanne-collins-jennifer-lawrence/ (June 3, 2011).

7   World Entertainment News Network, "Lawrence: 'I Have a Huge Responsibility to Play *Hunger Games* Heroine,' " March 20, 2011, also available online at http://www.hollywood.com/news/Lawrence_I_have_a_huge_responsibility_to_play_Hunger_Games_heroine/7775290 (August, 23, 2011).

8   Facebook, *Hunger Games* Official Facebook page, August 3, 2011, http://www.facebook.com/TheHungerGames (July 7, 2011).

8   Karen Valby, " 'The Hunger Games' Gets Its Girl," *Entertainment Weekly*, March 25, 2011, http://www.ew.com/ew/article/0,,20476091,00.html (June 3, 2011).

8–9   Franich, " 'Hunger Games': Suzanne Collins."

9   Josh Moss, "Too Young for Methods: Louisville's Academy Award-Nominated Actress Jennifer Lawrence," *Louisville Magazine*, February 9, 2011, http://www.louisville.com/content/too-young-methods-louisvilles-academy-award-nominated-actress-jennifer-lawrence-movies (June 23, 2011).

10   Ibid.

10   Chris Tinkham, "Jennifer Lawrence: Interview with the Star of *Winter's Bone*," *Under the Radar*, June 25, 2010, http://www.undertheradarmag.com/interviews/jennifer_lawrence/ (June 17, 2011).

13   Johanna Schneller, "Thanks for Raising Me, but I'm Going to Take It from Here," *Globe and Mail* (Toronto), June 11,

2010, http://www.theglobeandmail.com/news/arts/movies/
johanna-schneller/interview-with-winters-bone-star
-jennifer-lawrence/article1600683/ (June 3, 2011).

15 *Live! with Regis and Kelly*, "Jennifer Lawrence—*X-Men: First Class* Interview," June 10, 2011, http://www.youtube.com/watch?v=TcOMH1Wm-M4 (June 26, 2011).

15 Moss, "Too Young."

15 Jane Graham, "Jennifer Lawrence: A Shot of Kentucky Spirit," *Guardian* (Manchester), September 2, 2010, http://www.guardian.co.uk/film/2010/sep/02/jennifer-lawrence-sitting-pretty, (June 5, 2011).

16 Schneller, "Thanks for Raising Me."

16 World Entertainment News Network, "Lawrence Has Hunger Games Co-star to Thank for Her Career," May 20, 2011, also available online at http://www.pr-inside.com/lawrence-has-hunger-games-co-star-to-r2605923.htm (August 23, 2011).

16 Moss, "Too Young."

17 Danielle Nussbaum, "X Factor," *Teen Vogue*, May 2011, 110.

18–19 Jodie Foster, "Jennifer Lawrence," *Interview Magazine*, June 12, 2010, http://www.interviewmagazine.com/film/jennifer-lawrence/2/ (June 3, 2011).

20 Graham, "Jennifer Lawrence."

21 Ibid.

21 Jerry Rice, "Jennifer Lawrence: Cross-Country Fatigue Helped Give 'Bone' Its Leading Lady," *Daily Variety*, December 6, 2010, A4.

23 Steve Heisler, "Jennifer Lawrence: Crix Were Hot for Her Perf in Indie Release 'Winter's Bone,'" *Daily Variety*, October 15, 2010, A2.

23 Schneller, "Thanks for Raising Me."

23–24 Anthony Breznican, "'Winter's Bone' Star Back to Reality," *USA Today*, June 9, 2010.

24 Peter Travers, "Best Actress: It's Between Natalie Portman and Annette Bening," *Rolling Stone*, February 24, 2011, http://www.rollingstone.com/movies/blogs/the-travers-take/best-actress-its-between-natalie-portman-and-annette-bening-20110224 (June 3, 2011).

24 Joseph Lord, "Jennifer Lawrence: Bigger Things," *Louisville Courier-Journal*, October 14, 2009, http://louisville.metromix .com/movies/article/jennifer-lawrence-bigger-things/1535101/content (June 3, 2011).

24 Stephen Schaefer, "Jennifer Lawrence (Interview)," *Daily Variety*, October 25, 2010, A5.

25 Schneller, "Thanks for Raising Me."

25 *Live! with Regis and Kelly*, "Jennifer Lawrence."

26 Marlow Stern, "Jennifer Lawrence Is the Breakout Star of *Winter's Bone!*" *Manhattan Movie Magazine*, June 12, 2010, http://www.mahattanmoviemag.com (June 3, 2011).

27 Karen Valby, "The Chosen One," *Entertainment Weekly*, May 20, 2011, http://ew.com/ew/article/0,,2041995102.00.html (June 3, 2011).

27 Nussbaum, "X Factor," 110.

28 Jeremy Medina, "Jennifer Lawrence Dishes on 'Winter's Bone' and Stripping for 'Esquire,'" *Black Book*, June 28, 2010, http://www.blackbookmag.com/article/jennifer-lawrence/20149 (June 17, 2011).

29 Jean West, "Louisville Native's Film Career Continues to Soar with Golden Globe Nomination," Wave3.com, January 17, 2011, http://www.wave3.com/story/13855308/louisville-native-comes-close-to-winning-golden-globe (June 17, 2011).

29 Valby, "The Chosen One."

30 Jennifer Lawrence on *Jimmy Kimmel Live*, YouTube.com, (uploaded by JimmyKimmelLive on January 18, 2011), http://www.youtube.com/watch?v=qAfUs2Bpo5M&feature =related (June 17, 2011).

30–31 Jen Chaney, "Louisville's Jennifer Lawrence Can Barely Keep Up with Her Own Success," *Washington Post*, June 2, 2011.

31 Facebook, Jennifer Lawrence page, June 25, 2011, http://www.facebook.com/JenniferLawrence?sk=wall&filter=12 (July 3, 2011).

31 Jen Chaney, "Louisville's Jennifer Lawrence Can Barely Keep up with Her Own Success," *Washington Post*, June 2, 2011.

32 Kara Warner, with reporting by Josh Horowitz, "Jennifer Lawrence Talks Training to Play Katniss Everdeen in 'Hunger Games,'" MTV News, May 25, 2011, http://www.mtv.com/news/articles/1664588/jennifer-lawrence-katniss-everdeen-hunger-games.jhtml (August 22, 2011).

33 Rick Margolis, "A Killer Story: An Interview with Suzanne Collins, Author of 'The Hunger Games,'" *School Library Journal*, September 1, 2008, http://www.schoollibraryjournal.com/article/CA6590063.html (June 20, 2011).

34–35 Kara Warner, "Exclusive: Jennifer Lawrence Officially Cast in 'Hunger Games,'" MTV.com, March 17, 2011, http://www.mtv.com/news/articles/1660152/jennifer-lawrence-hunger-games.jhtml (June 3, 2011).

35 Valby, "The Chosen One."

45 World Entertainment News Network, "Lawrence: 'I Have a Huge Responsibility.'"

46 Karen Valby, "'The Hunger Games': Jennifer Lawrence Defends Her Peeta and Gale," *Entertainment Weekly*, May 20, 2011, http://insidemovies.ew (June 3, 2011).

46–47 Ibid.

38 Warner, with Horowitz, "Jennifer Lawrence."

39 David Katz, "You Have Now Heard of Jennifer Lawrence: A Woman We Love," *Esquire*, June–July 2010, 138.

39 Stern, "Jennifer Lawrence."

39 Lord, "Jennifer Lawrence."

39 Schneller, "Thanks for Raising Me."

SELECTED BIBLIOGRAPHY

Chaney, Jen. "Louisville's Jennifer Lawrence Can Barely Keep Up with Her Own Success." *Washington Post*, June 2, 2011.

Franich, Darren. "' Hunger Games': Suzanne Collins Talks Jennifer Lawrence as Katniss—EXCLUSIVE." *Entertainment Weekly*. 2011. http://insidemovies.ew.com/2011/03/21/hunger-games-suzanne-collins-jennifer-lawrence/ (June 3, 2011).

Graham, Jane. "Jennifer Lawrence: A Shot of Kentucky Spirit." *Guardian* (Manchester), September 2, 2010. http://www.guardian.co.uk/film/2010/sep/02/jennifer-lawrence-sitting-pretty (June 5, 2011).

Moss, Josh. "Too Young for Methods: Louisville's Academy Award-Nominated Actress Jennifer Lawrence." *Louisville Magazine*, February 9, 2011. http://www.louisville.com/content/too-young-methods-louisvilles-academy-award-nominated-actress-jennifer-lawrence-movies (June 23, 2011).

Nussbaum, Danielle. "X Factor." *Teen Vogue*, May 2011, 110.

Rice, Jerry. "Jennifer Lawrence: Cross-Country Fatigue Helped Give 'Bone' Its Leading Lady." *Daily Variety*, December 6, 2010, A4.

Schneller, Johanna. "Thanks for Raising Me, but I'm Going to Take It from Here." *Globe and Mail* (Toronto), June 11, 2010. http://www.theglobeandmail.com/news/arts/movies/johanna-schneller/interview-with-winters-bone-star-jennifer-lawrence/article1600683/ (June 3, 2011).

Valby, Karen. "'The Hunger Games' Gets Its Girl." *Entertainment Weekly*, March 25, 2011. http://www.ew.com/ew/article/0,,20476091,00.html (June 3, 2011).

FURTHER READING

BOOKS

Collins, Suzanne. *The Hunger Games*. New York: Scholastic Press, 2008.

Krohn, Katherine. *Stephenie Meyer: Dreaming of* Twilight. Minneapolis: Twenty-First Century Books, 2011.

Wilson, Leah, ed. *The Girl Who Was on Fire: Your Favorite Authors on Suzanne Collins'* Hunger Games *Trilogy*. Dallas: BenBella Books, 2011.

WEBSITES

IMDb: Jennifer Lawrence
   http://www.imdb.com/name/nm2225369
   Check out Jennifer Lawrence's profile on the Internet Movie Database.

Suzanne Collins
   http://www.suzannecollinsbooks.com
   Visit the official website of the author of *The Hunger Games* trilogy.

INDEX